Hi Dad

Best Wishes for
your 87th Birthday
Hope there are many
more
            Love
            Marg.

二丁才亦永

Echoes from the Orient

Echoes from the Orient

Wisdom of *Lao-Tse*

With Parallels in

Western Thought

Selected by Robert Wood

♔ Hallmark Editions

The sayings of Lao-Tse appear
in letters of this style.

The parallel western thoughts
appear in this style of lettering
with their authors' names.

Without stirring abroad
One can know the whole world;
Without looking out of the window
One can see
the way of heaven.

To see a world in a grain of sand

And a heaven in a wild flower:

Hold infinity in the palm of your hand,

And eternity in an hour.

William Blake

The way of truth

      is like a great highway.

It is not hard to find.

                 Mencius

Were I

possessed of the least knowledge,

I would,

when walking of the great way,

fear only paths that lead astray.

The great way

is easy,

yet people prefer by-paths.

Between yea and nay

How much difference is there?

Between good and evil

How great is the distance?

There is not the thickness of a sixpence

between good and evil.

Thomas Fuller

Stay alert — stay alive.

American soldiers' saying

It is by being alive to difficulty
that one can avoid it.
The sage
meets with no difficulty.
It is because
he is alive to it
that he meets
with no difficulty.

It is the way of heaven
to show no favoritism.
It is forever
on the side of the good man.

All things work together for good

to them that love God.

Romans 8:28 (KJV)

Be content with such things as ye have.

Hebrews 13:5 (KJV)

Bring it about

    that the people will return

to the use of the knotted rope,

Will find relish in their food

    And beauty in their clothes,

Will be content in their abode

       And happy

    in the way they live.

Straightforward words

        Seem paradoxical.

There are times

    when truth

hardly seems probable.

Nicolas Boileau

One should keep to

old roads and old friends.

German proverb

Let your wheels move
along old ruts.
This is known as
mysterious sameness.

The spirit of the valley never dies.

This is called the mysterious female.

The gateway

of the mysterious female

Is called the root of heaven and earth.

Dimly visible,

it seems as if it were there,

Yet use will never drain it.

WOMAN: You are the gates of the body,

and you are the gates of the soul.

Walt Whitman

Should a wise man

utter vain knowledge,

and fill his belly

with the east wind?

Job 15:2 (KJV)

To use words but rarely

        Is to be natural.

Hence a gusty wind

    cannot last all morning,

    and a sudden downpour

    cannot last all day.

There is no crime greater
  than having too many desires;
There is no disaster greater
  than not being content;
There is no misfortune greater
  than being covetous.
Hence in being content,
  one will always have enough.

A great soul

prefers moderation to excess.

Seneca

War is death's feast.

Thomas Hobbes

Where troops have encamped
            There will brambles grow;
In the wake of a mighty army
  Bad harvests follow without fail.

He who tiptoes cannot stand;

   he who strides cannot walk.

He who shows himself

         is not conspicuous;

He who considers himself right

    is not illustrious;

He who brags will have no merit;

He who boasts will not endure.

God resisteth the proud, but giveth

grace unto the humble.

James 4:6 (KJV)

War is as much

a punishment to the punisher

as to the sufferer.

Thomas Jefferson

When great numbers
  of people are killed,
one should weep over them
      with sorrow.
When victorious in war,
  one should observe
  the rites of mourning.

Hold fast to the way of antiquity
In order to keep in control
of the realm today.
The ability to know
the beginning of antiquity
Is called the thread
running through the way.

He that would know what shall be,

must consider what hath been.

Henry Bohn

The truth hurts.

Old English Proverb

Truthful words

are not beautiful.

Some things lead and some follow;
   Some breathe gently
      and some breathe hard;
Some are strong and some are weak;
   Some destroy
      and some are destroyed.

When two men ride on a horse,

one must ride behind.

William Shakespeare

But many that are first shall be last;

and the last shall be first.

Matthew 19:30 (KJV)

Is not the way of heaven
like the stretching of a bow?
   The high it presses down,
   The low it lifted up;
  The excessive it takes from,
    The deficient it gives to.

A tree that can fill the span
    of a man's arms
        Grows from a downy tip;
A terrace nine storeys high
    Rises from hodfuls of earth;
A journey of a thousand miles
    Starts from beneath one's feet.

Little drops of water,

    little grains of sand

Make the mighty ocean

    and the pleasant land.

Julia F. Carney

Never put off till tomorrow

what you can do today.

Lord Chesterfield

It is easy to break a thing
   when it is yet brittle;
It is easy to dissolve a thing
   when it is yet minute.
Deal with a thing
       while it is still nothing;
Keep a thing in order
   before disorder sets in.

Heaven and earth
are enduring.

One generation passeth away,

and another generation cometh:

but the earth abideth for ever.

Ecclesiastes 1:4 (KJV)

The Chinese figure
appearing in this book means *eternity*
and is made up
of the eight basic strokes
of all Chinese calligraphy.
The quotations of Lao-Tse
are set in Codex,
a calligraphic roman face
designed by Georg Trump.
Western quotations are set in Optima,
a roman face of graceful simplicity
designed by Hermann Zapf.
The paper is
Hallmark Crown-Pearl paper.